Recorder Magic
Book 2

By David Moses and Jane Sebba

A & C Black • London

www.recordermagic.co.uk

cabbage crazy

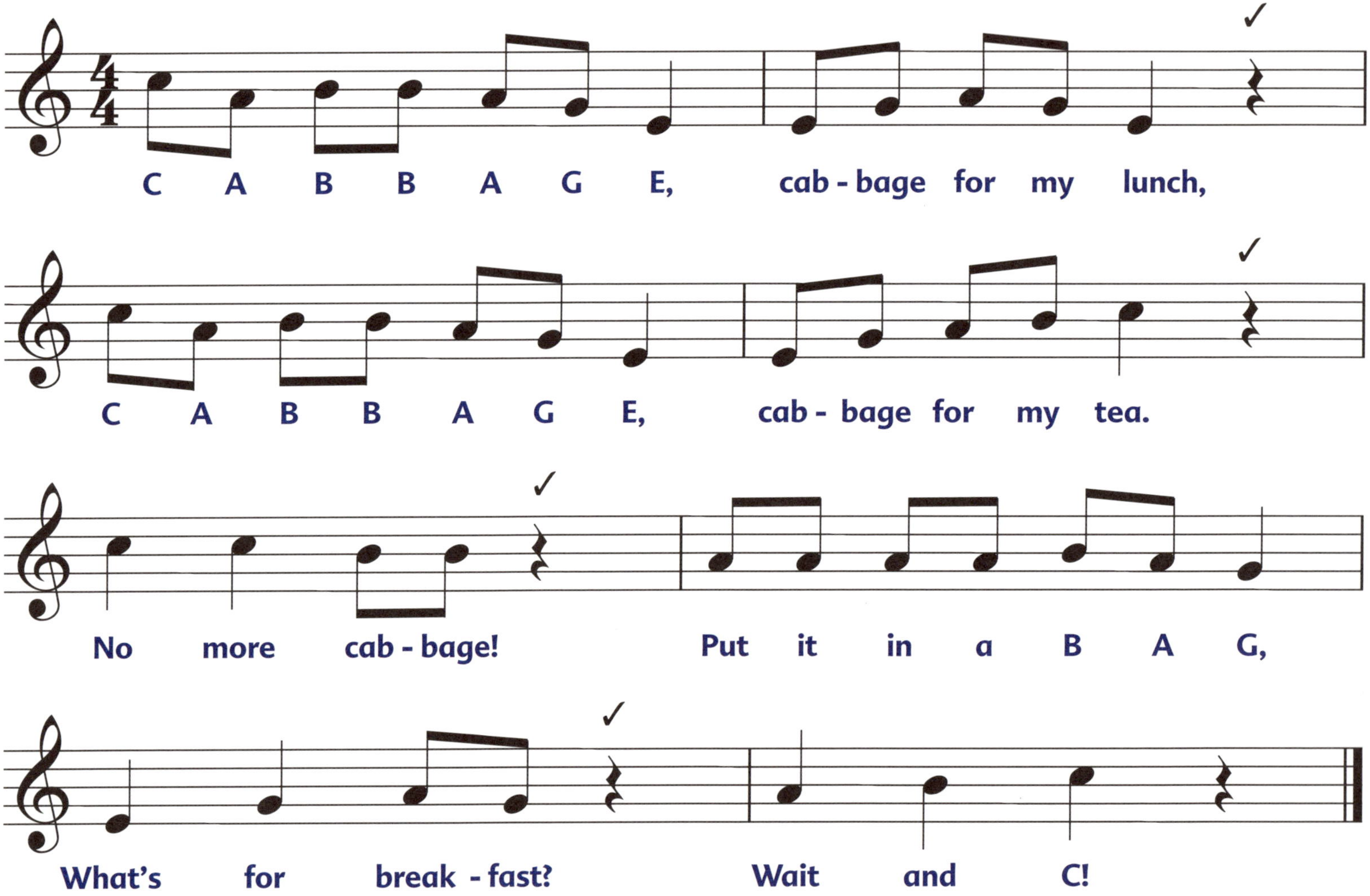

C A B B A G E, cab - bage for my lunch,

C A B B A G E, cab - bage for my tea.

No more cab - bage! Put it in a B A G,

What's for break - fast? Wait and C!

Dotted notes

A note with a dot after it is lengthened by half of its value.

dotted minim = minim + crotchet

= <u>three beats</u>

dotted crotchet = crotchet+quaver

= <u>one and a half beats</u>

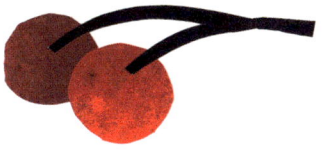

Feeling fruity

Eat - ing all the fruit in the kit - chen,

Eat all the fruit in the street.

Nice_____ and sweet, a jui - cy treat.

Lots of fruit to eat.

Make up fruity word patterns of your own to fit the rhythm of the two bars in the box, eg

Sliced ba-na - na, jui - cy peach.
Cris - py ap - ple, pur - ple plum.

3

The Bellipong
(duet with *The Zippi*)

- Play these pieces one after the other.
- Then play them at the same time with a friend. Start at the same time and play at the same crotchet speed. Don't forget the repeat in *The Zippi*.

Fat and round, the Bel - li - pong is slow, His

tum - my wob - bles low, on - ly just off the ground.

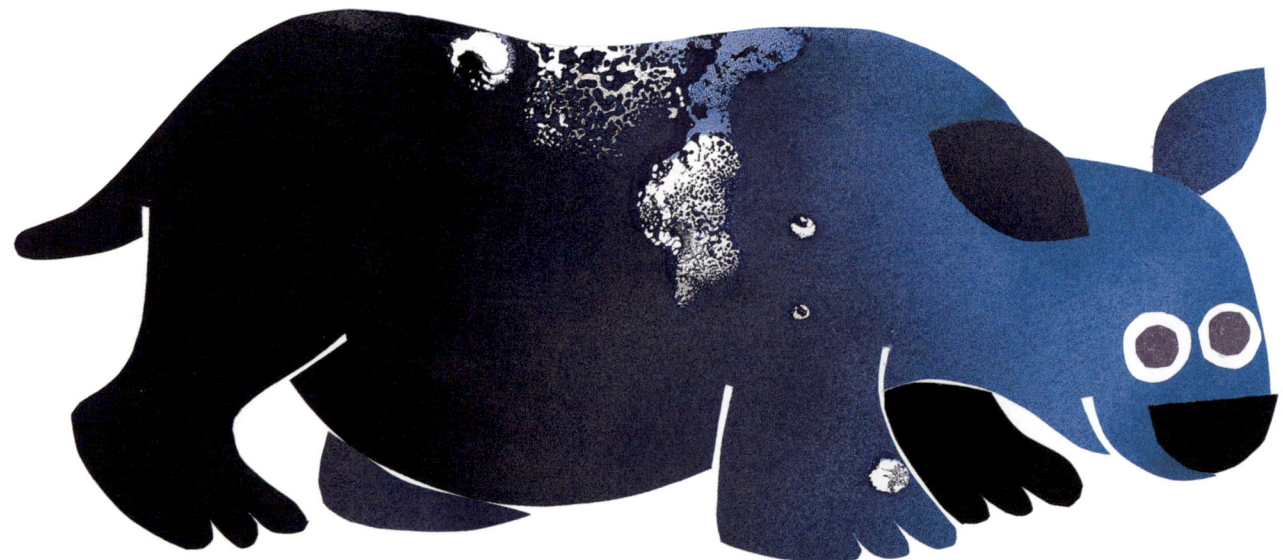

4

Question: what do you notice about these two pieces?

The Zippi
(duet with *The Bellipong*)

Thin   and long,   the Zip - pi whiz - zes past,   She's

go - ing twice as fast   as the old   Bel - li - pong.

Answer: the pieces use the same notes, but they are twice as long in *The Bellipong*.

www.recordermagic.co.uk

New note high D

High D is played with the second finger of the left hand only.

Fanfare for high D (duet)

High D ho

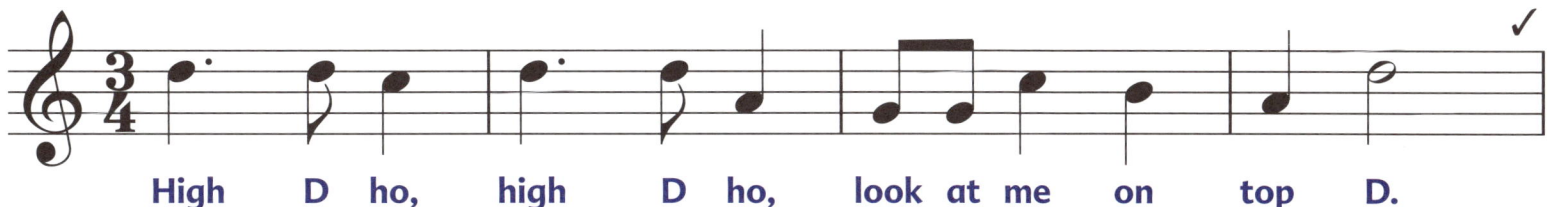

High D ho, high D ho, look at me on top D.

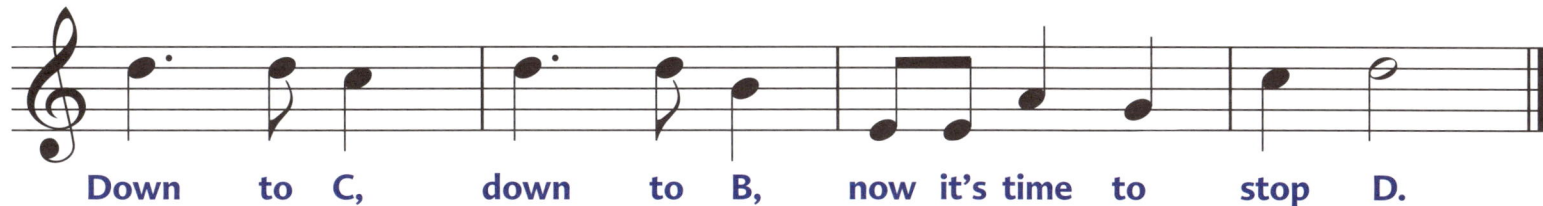

Down to C, down to B, now it's time to stop D.

Sorry and sad

I'm sor - ry to say that I don't want to play, I'm

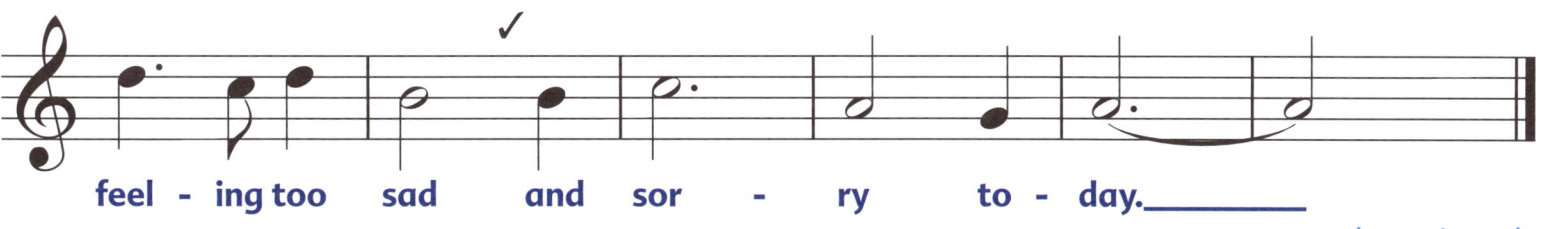

feel - ing too sad and sor - ry to - day._____

www.recordermagic.co.uk

Staccato

Staccato means short and detached.

A dot below or above a note tells you to play it staccato. Shorten the note to about half its usual length by moving your tongue back quickly and neatly behind your top front teeth to stop the breath.

Practise playing these notes staccato before learning the piece.

Make the notes short and light.

Shortcake

Short - cake, short sight, make the notes short and light,

Short sleeves, short hair, no long notes, just lots of air!

www.recordermagic.co.uk

Pelican pecked a pea
(duet with *Merrily we roll along*)

• These two pieces can be played at the same time as a duet.
• Notice that *Pelican pecked a pea* starts one crotchet beat before *Merrily we roll along*.

A pe - li - can pecked a pea, and said, with glee, 'They're hard for a bird like me to e - ven see.'

Merrily we roll along
(duet with *Pelican pecked a pea*)

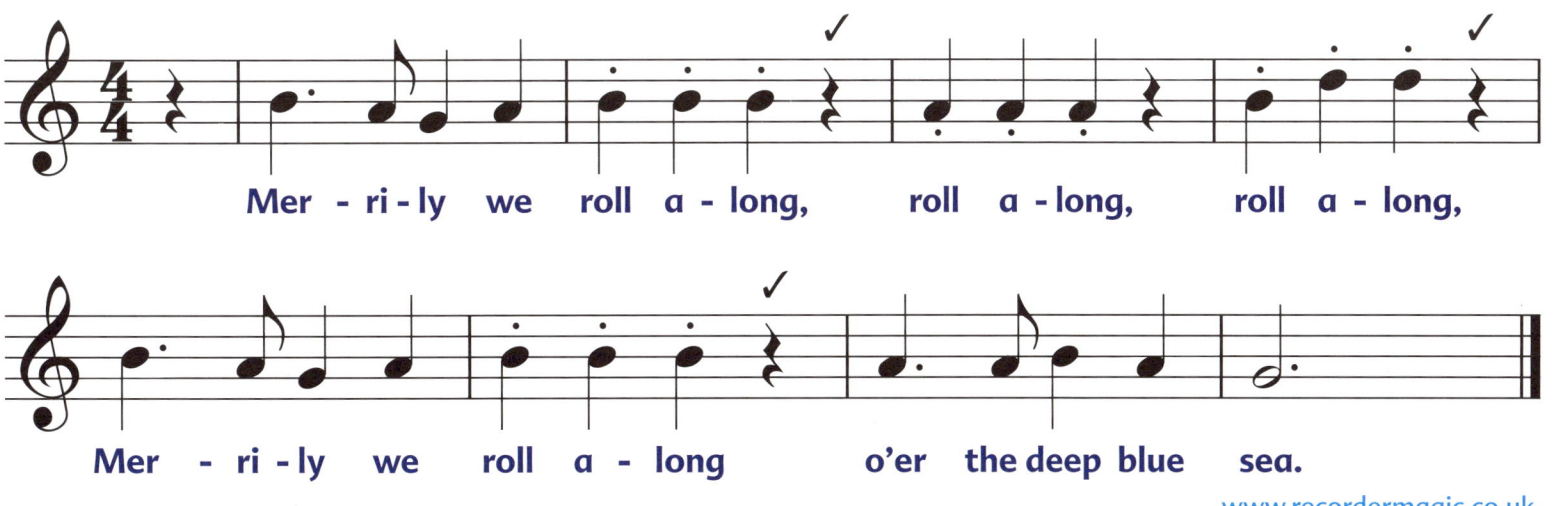

Mer - ri - ly we roll a - long, roll a - long, roll a - long, Mer - ri - ly we roll a - long o'er the deep blue sea.

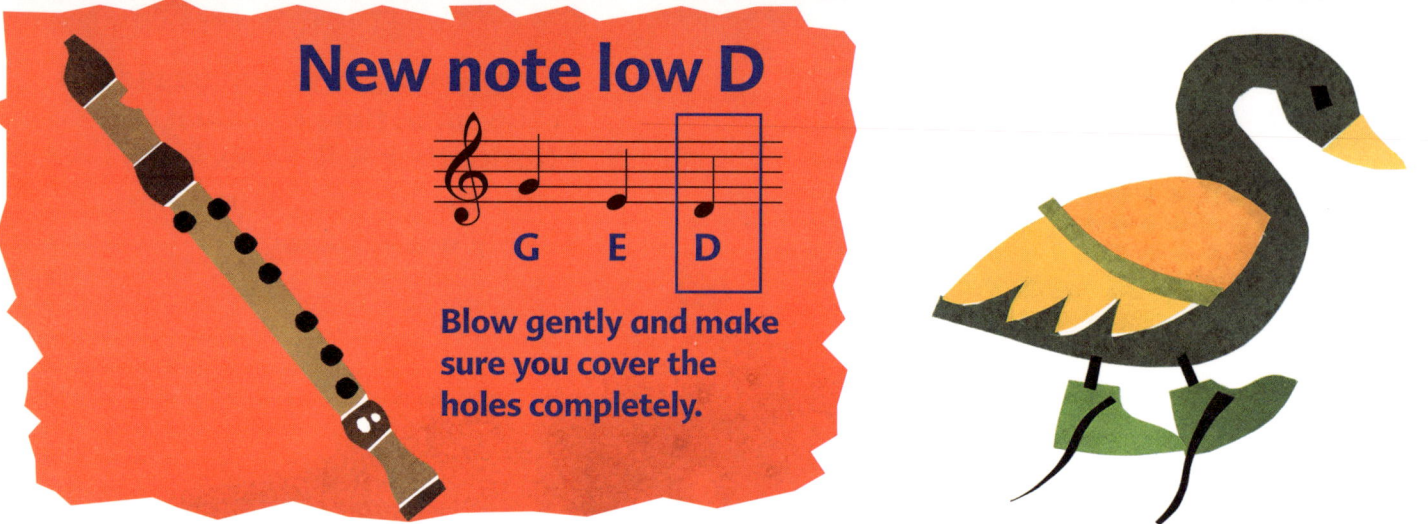

New note low D

G E D

Blow gently and make sure you cover the holes completely.

Waking from dreams

Day breaks the ma - gic of a dream,

Just like the rip - ples in a stream.

Steps

Four steps, five steps, six steps, run-ning on the spot,

Three steps, four steps, five steps, get-ting ve - ry hot.

Going to the fair (duet)

Me, Rav - i, go - ing to the fair,

Mol - ly, Ol - ly, with a

cat rat chi-cken on a chair. whoop whis-tle

and a and a We can we can we can

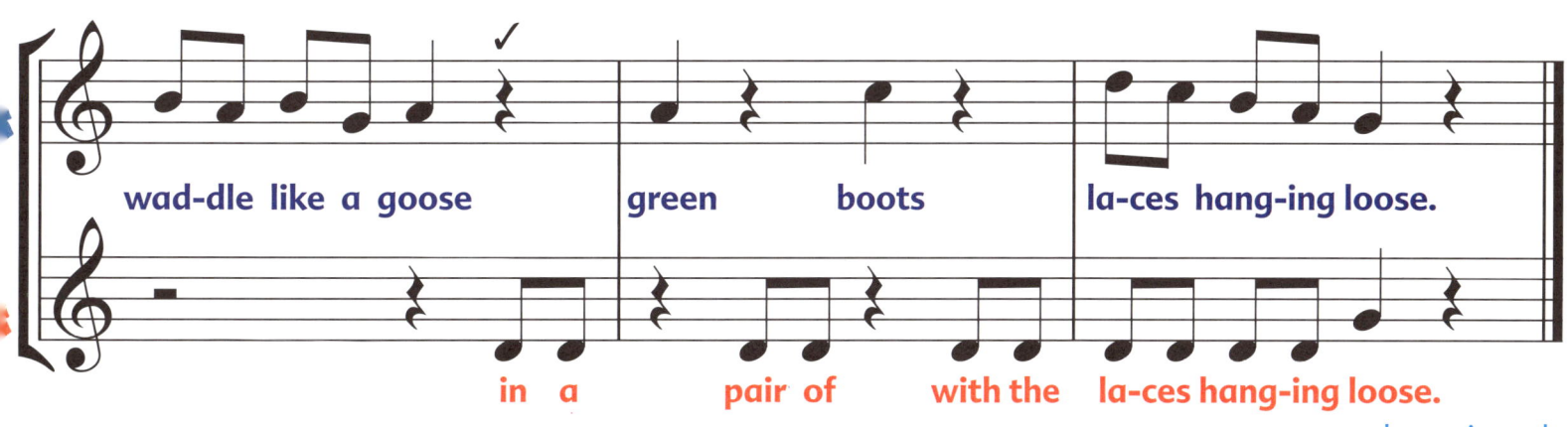

wad-dle like a goose green boots la-ces hang-ing loose.

in a pair of with the la-ces hang-ing loose.

www.recordermagic.co.uk

The toucan

Few   can   do   what   a   tou - can   can,

Eat   spa - ghet - ti   from   a   fry - ing   pan,

Tied   to   a   tree   in   the   mid - dle   of   the   sea.   If   a

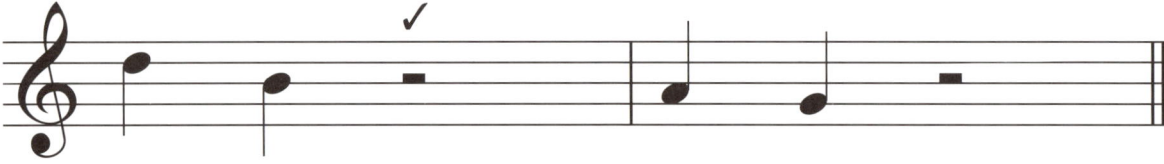

tou - can,   you   can.

www.recordermagic.co.uk

Ola, Ola (duet)

O - la, O - la, give us a tune played up - on your big bas-soon.

My tune's chir - py, yours is broad, it fits with my re - cor - der.

Time signature

6 ← Six
8 ← quaver beats in a bar.

The six quavers

♪ ♪ ♪ ♪ ♪ ♪

are counted in two groups of three,

or as two dotted crotchets.

No nonsense

• Clap and say these rhythms: **6**
8

Hig - gle - dy	pig - gle - dy

bot - tle	of	pop,

half	a	cake	with

cher - ries	on	top.

Brett	met	the

man	in	the	moon,	who

ate	the	cake	with	a

fork	and	spoon.

Bottle of pop

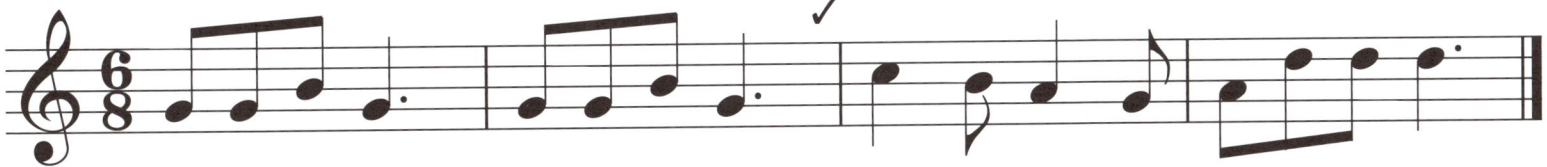

Bot - tle of pop,   bot - tle of pop,   half   a   cake with cher-ries on top.

The man in the moon

Brett   met   the   man in the moon, who   ate   the cake with a   fork   and spoon.

Higgledy piggledy (round)

* Second part starts here.

Hig-gle-dy pig-gle-dy hig-gle-dy pig-gle-dy half   a   pac-ket of   pop - corn.

Half a cake

Make up the tune here yourself.

Half   a   cake   is   bet-ter than none, but   all of the cake is much more fun.

www.recordermagic.co.uk

Nursery rhyme mix-up

Oh dear, what can the mat-ter be?

Jack and Jill fell up the hill!

Lit-tle Jack Hor-ner went to a sau-na and

came home a-gain feel-ing ill.

funky chunky monkey

www.recordermagic.co.uk

Catch me if you can (duet/trio)

This piece can be played as a duet. To make it into a trio, ask another friend or group to play the ostinato.

Optional ostinato

Play this bar eight times:

Then play this bar to finish:

www.recordermagic.co.uk

Slur

A slur connecting two different notes tells you to move smoothly from one to the other.
Tongue the first note only and carry on blowing as you move your fingers to the second note.

Practise slurring these pairs of notes before learning *Irish air*.

Irish air

Gently

The owl and the cuckoo (duet)

Chirpy

Tu - whit, tu - whit, tu - whoo._____ Tu - whit, tu -

Cuck - oo!

- whit, tu - whoo._____ Tu - whit, tu - whoo, tu - whit, tu -

Cuck - oo!

- whoo, tu - whit, tu - whit, tu - whoo._____

Cuck - oo!

First and second time bars

| 1. | 2. |

**The first time you play the last section of the piece, play the first time bar.
The second time you play this section, miss out the first time bar and end with the second time bar.**

Skye boat song

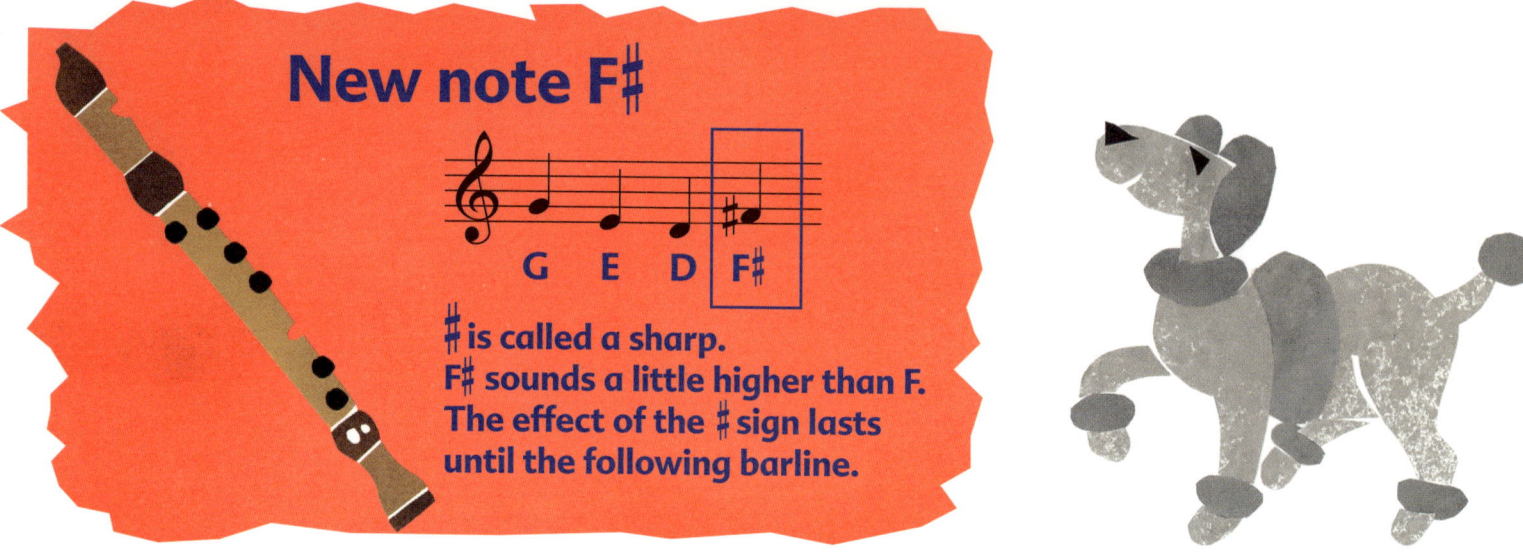

New note F♯

G E D F♯

♯ is called a sharp.
F♯ sounds a little higher than F.
The effect of the ♯ sign lasts
until the following barline.

Out for a walk

At a walking pace

Poodles

Carefully

Seagulls (duet)

Delicately

Sea - gulls cry-ing,___   Sea - gulls fly - ing___

Sea-gulls swoop-ing low   close to my hat,___   **1.** What was that?

2. That went splat!

Blow gently into the top section of your recorder.

Blow a raspberry into the other end.

• Swap parts when you repeat the piece.

23

Old Joe Clark

Neatly

The keel row (duet)

Playfully

Rhino march

Slow and steady

Twinkling stars

Gracefully

Key signature

The ♯ sign at the beginning of the stave means that every F should be played as an F♯.

Bobby Shaftoe

Smoothly

Look sharp, look lively (duet)

Very rhythmic

Look sharp, look live - ly, look sad, look bad, look cold and lost, look

Look sharp, look live - ly, look sad, look bad, look cold and

smug, look grum-py, look left, look right be - fore you cross. Look

lost, look smug, look grum-py, look left, look right be - fore you

sharp, look live - ly, look af - ter your - self.

cross. Look sharp, look live - ly, look af - ter your - self.

www.recordermagic.co.uk

Wobbly bicycles (duet)

Neatly

Congratulations! You've nearly finished book 2. Visit www.recordermagic.co.uk to find out about your fantastic free certificate.

Make the *toot* sound using this fingering and by blowing a little harder than usual.

Train

Rhythmically

Train comes hur - tl - ing down the track,   Toot,   toot,   toot toot toot.

Com - ing here be - fore go - ing back,   Toot,   toot,   toot toot toot.

Blow that whis - tle   loud and strong,   Ev - 'ry - bo - dy can hear   its song,

Train   comes hur - tl - ing down the track,   Toot,   toot,   toot toot toot.

Com - ing here be - fore   go - ing back,   Toot!_____

Bear dance

Slow and heavy

www.recordermagic.co.uk

Notes learnt

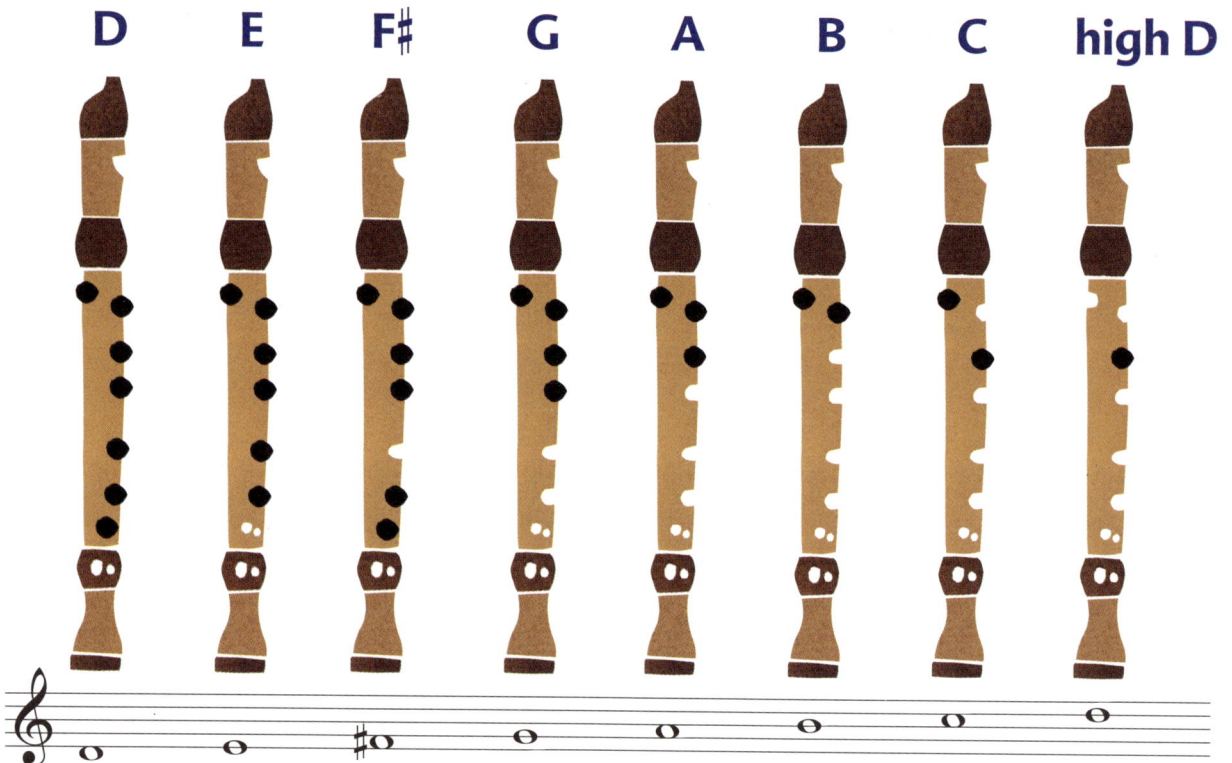

D   E   F♯   G   A   B   C   high D

Acknowledgements

The authors and publishers would like to thank all the recorder teachers who assisted in the preparation of this book: Mary Albrighton, Beverley Ann Atherton, Jane Ayles, Sheena Billett, Anne Brooks, Sue Coates, Kate Collings, Mrs S. Dean, Lesley Dolphin, Angela D'Silva, Ann H. Duthie, Anita Felton, Sarah Gardner, Lindsey Giles, Paul Gregory, Avril Grigg, Valerie Henry, Barbara Honeyball, Marta Howard, Chris Jaggard, Carmel Kelly, Sue Klein, Hilary Littlewood, Linda Morse, Judith Mumby, Hilary Oliver, Chris Parrett, Helen Pearce, Catharine Perrin, Ann Sharman, Jeanne Simpson, Anne Snowden, Odette Stephenson, Elaine Sutton, Clare Talbot, Kathleen Thomas, Chris Treggiden, Nicola Walsh and Felicity Ward-Smith.

Special thanks are due to the following consultants: Tom Deveson, Mary Edwards, Linda Evans, Jenny Fisher, Dot Fraser, Grace Gallagher, Maureen Hanke, Derek Kitt, Helen MacGregor, Sue Nicholls, Sheena Roberts, Angela Rodriguez, Liz Stock and Marie Tomlinson.

Thanks also to Tessa Montague for modelling the recorder positions for the illustrator.

First published 2001
by A & C Black (Publishers) Ltd
37, Soho Square
London
W1D 3QZ
© 2001 A & C Black (Publishers) Ltd

Edited by Ana Sanderson and Emily Haward
Music setting by Emily Haward
Illustrations by Alison Dexter
Designed by Dorothy Moir
Printed in Hong Kong by Wing King Tong Co Ltd.
ISBN 0 7136 5143 1

www.recordermagic.co.uk